Changing Gears®

Mark Dando with Doug Richardson

SilverWood

Published in 2022 by SilverWood Books

SilverWood Books Ltd
14 Small Street, Bristol, BS1 1DE, United Kingdom
www.silverwoodbooks.co.uk

Copyright © Mark Dando 2022
Images and Illustrations © Mark Dando 2022

ISBN 978-1-80042-190-5 (paperback)
ISBN 978-1-80042-191-2 (ebook)

British Library Cataloguing in Publication Data
A CIP catalogue record for this book is available from the British Library

Page design and typesetting by SilverWood Books

MARK DANDO is an author, a mentor, coach and trainer.

He works with a small team of highly talented developers: Doug Richardson, Alison Rogers, Andrew Manuel and Luke Thomas.

He co-founded what became Coloured Square Limited with Doug in 2000. Their provocative and powerful "structured common-sense" system of learning and development continues to receive rave reviews from individuals and organisations who want help to improve their management, leadership, sales, influence, presenting – in short anything which requires more skill in communication. Their favourite brief is to help organisations change their approach to the business of learning and development itself – improving speed to competence and engagement. They've been changing gears for 20 years.

Mark has been an author since 2013. This is his fifth personal development book. His first three were about attitudes to Time, attitudes to Presenting, and the attitudes and activities required to improve personal well-being and resilience. His fourth, *Coach-Sell-Teach-Tell*™ published in May 2020, was a plea for managers and developers to increase the amount and effectiveness of development they provide their people by making better choices about the attitudes and approaches they use. He has published two children's books: *The Boy Who Yawned*, and *The Boy Who Kidnapped Father Christmas*.

In 2019 Mark became a poet. He can be seen and heard performing at spoken word events in Bristol and Bath on a regular basis.

When he's not writing, developing people or performing poetry, he continues to learn guitar (very slowly), practises Tai Chi, and indulges in games of all kinds.

He lives in Bristol.

To find out more visit the Coloured Square website at www.colouredsquare.com

Also by Mark Dando

Don't Strain LittleBrain

Also by Mark Dando and Doug Richardson

Squeeze Your Time

Kill the Robot

Also by Mark Dando with Doug Richardson

Coach-Sell-Teach-Tell

Children's books by Mark Dando

The Boy Who Yawned

The Boy Who Kidnapped Father Christmas

Contents

Introduction: Autopilot

Imagine setting a vehicle to autopilot – like setting your car to cruise control or self-drive. Now imagine it malfunctions – gets stuck in one gear – and you don't notice. Maybe you're too busy thinking about something, listening to the radio or talking on the phone. As a result, you don't realise that your car never speeds up, never slows down, never changes gears. Maybe you don't notice because you feel very comfortable at this one speed.

I always travel at 60mph – it's just how I am!

How long would it be before you crashed?

It might be quite some time – you might be fine for hours, for hundreds of miles. There's nothing wrong with being in one gear only. As long as that gear is the right one for the terrain, for your speed, for the driving conditions and for the reactions of other drivers.

But on some journeys, you'll be in trouble almost immediately – at the first corner. You'll be in trouble because your vehicle should have changed down a gear or two in order to cope with the change in the situation, the environment or other drivers.

In our work as coaches and trainers over the last twenty years we've seen this autopilot behaviour on a regular basis – but we're not talking about roads and cars. We're talking behaviours in meetings, in presentations, in conversations, in performance reviews, in coaching: people who insist on doing particular things in one gear:

- the gear they always use when speaking to direct reports
- the gear they always use to speak to their boss
- the gear they use when they're talking to their child or one of their parents
- the gear they like to present or coach in
- the gear they automatically teach in.

And on a regular basis we get to watch while they crash. They crash their meeting. They crash their presentation. They crash into other people.

Sometimes it's an immediate and obvious crash – it's apparent to everyone (even to themselves) that they're in the wrong gear, even though, sadly, they don't seem to be able to do anything about it. Sometimes it's only a small bump instead of a crash.

Sometimes it's not obvious at all – it's more like a slow-motion crash, taking its time, happening over a number of interactions in ways too difficult for anyone to notice and realise. Crashing communications. Crashing the management of their team. Crashing their relationships with their boss, their stakeholders, their loved ones.

This book is for you if you'd like to explore a change of gears so that you can:

- improve your influence
- mend relationships that just don't seem to be working well
- get your message across better.

Or perhaps you'd just like to crash yourself less…

Chapter One

What Do We Mean By Gears?

When we talk about gears, we're talking about a particular set of behaviours that fit together somehow. Often you don't have to think about them – you just slip into them automatically because of the situation or the people involved.

Picture going to the pub to meet a group of friends. At the door to the pub, you don't think about how you'll need to behave with them. You know already the collection of behaviours you'll use. It's not something you need to make a conscious decision about.

Picture going into your boss's office. At the office door, you might have to think a little about how you'll behave with them. But, if you're familiar with them, it'll only take a second; you'll know the collection of behaviours you need to use – it's probably not the collection of behaviours you use in the pub with your friends.

Gears are collections or sets of behaviours that seem to go together. Sometimes you slip into them naturally because of the moment or the situation – often not consciously.

On TV last night, a politician was being interviewed. Through the whole 40-minute exchange, the interviewer used one collection of behaviours – one gear. You'll be familiar with the kind of interview we're talking about. We'd describe the interviewer's behaviours as: fast, impatient, loud, questioning, interrupting, talking over, frowning, unsmiling and cold.

In comparison, the politician's behaviours were: slow, insistent, loud, evasive, interrupting, talking over, frowning, smiling and warm.

The interview wasn't great – we didn't find out much at all about what the politician really thought. Both interviewer and interviewee seemed to have preselected a particular set of behaviours (a gear as we'll call it) and each stayed fixed in that set of behaviours for the full duration of the interview – whether or not the interview was going well (and it wasn't).

This book is about the idea that if we followed you around and filmed you for a while as you talked with your boss, talked with your partner, talked to a customer, made a presentation, ran a meeting, etc., there's a good chance we might record you also preselecting a set of behaviours – a gear – which you then stay fixed in for the duration of each interaction, whether or not it seemed to be working. In fact, there's a small possibility that several times you preselected the same gear, or at least a very small collection of gears, for a number of these interactions.

This book is designed to help you begin to notice when you get fixed in a gear that clearly isn't working (but you're tempted to stay fixed in it anyway).

It's about the simple idea that you have a number of gears (a number of sets of behaviours) that you naturally know how to use, but, for some reason, you don't always know when to use them and for how long.

It's about developing more awareness of the gears you use. It's about using a couple of simple disciplines to bring your attention to these gears so that you're more able to use them when you need to. These disciplines are called 'Pre-Check' and 'Time Out'. More about them later.

It's also about the gaps between your existing gears. Noticing the gaps where, for whatever reason, you don't use certain sets of behaviours, which would help you in some situations.

Whenever we tell people about this simple idea of changing gears, it seems to help them (sometimes profoundly) to plan for and deliver the right kinds of behaviours to suit the situation that they're in.

Ultimately, we hope this book will enable you to get yourself, or a situation, unstuck.

Chapter Two

Reasons to Change Gears

We're going to think about four specific reasons to change gears. There will be others, but this is where our focus will be for much of the book.

Connection: getting in rapport with someone so you're productive together.

Personal impact: behaving in a manner designed to make things happen, create change, influence, etc. (being less concerned with staying connected).

Promoting alertness and interest *in others*: difference fires the brain chemicals of alertness. To create and maintain interest, variation of behaviour is useful.

Promoting alertness and interest *in yourself*: as in others, varying your behaviours will maintain your own levels of interest and productivity.

Let's look at each of these in turn.

Connection Often cited as being at the heart of influence, it's also the basis of a good relationship. It's about speaking, moving and thinking in ways that give the other person the sense that "you're my kind of person". Not because they agree with everything you say, but because the way you're doing things and the way you're saying things is somehow similar to the habitual way in which they like doing and saying things – and therefore it appeals to them.

Good connection is formed when you adjust your behaviours slightly to be a little more like the other person's behaviours or so your behaviours complement theirs in an appropriate manner (you follow them). As you connect, they respond – unconsciously adjusting *their* behaviours now so that their pace, tone, intensity and movements are more like yours (they follow you). Usually this all happens unconsciously, but when a relationship isn't going well, we can use this principle more consciously.

This is rapport – the word comes from the French *en rapport*, meaning "in connection". It doesn't mean you like each other; it doesn't mean you're friends. It just means you feel connected enough to be productive together somehow (friendship may well follow, but it doesn't have to).

Personal impact This is about your need to push or pull people into a different state, but where you're less concerned with creating a connection. Maybe you already have it or maybe you're not concerned with connection at all on this occasion, because you feel more 'in charge' somehow and the other person just needs to follow you. This could be, for example, because you want more enthusiasm from them, you want more get-up-and-go, you want them to realise that you need some action. It could be because you need to lead them in a particular direction. It could even be for reasons of health and safety or well-being, etc. In these situations, your gear-change isn't about getting a connection; it's about setting the pace, tone, energy and intensity *you* want. This is personal impact. And, of course, this pace, tone, energy and intensity that *you* want isn't always greater – it isn't always an increase. It may be that you need to be slower, quieter, gentler or less intense in order to create change in the situation or person.

Promoting alertness and interest in others Sometimes you need to create or maintain interest in order to make things happen or just to make sure people listen and hear what you're saying. If we're not really captivated by the words someone's saying (the content), then when they speak with one speed, tone or intensity, using the same movements, it doesn't take long for our thinking brain to begin to drift off in search of novelty and interest.

Your prefrontal cortex – your thinking brain – enjoys a hit of a neurochemical called dopamine to reawaken its alertness and its interest. This hit of dopamine is prompted by novelty (among other things), so changing gears when communicating is very helpful to keep people's attention. It really isn't just what you say; it's the way that you say it. And if you say it too much the same way throughout your communication, well, then you run the risk of your listener or your audience switching off.

Promoting alertness and interest in yourself If you get stuck in one set of behaviours, hunched over at your desk, writing a report, analysing data or proofreading your latest book, then unless you're particularly fascinated by the content involved, pretty soon your prefrontal cortex can go to sleep, simply because you yourself are too static and samey. A different gear would help you to stay productive throughout the day.

Some people start talking out loud to themselves to do this. Some take a regular walk to the kettle and back. Some change the music they're listening to. All of these kinds of things are used to change your state so that you can stay interested enough and productive, so that you can get yourself moving, get on with a piece of work, work faster – whatever. Even here, when trying to change your own state, it can help to have a set of gears available to you – a set of behaviours you already know, but which you won't use without a direct instruction to yourself, willing yourself into them. A sense of your gears will help you with this; it'll give you a language with which to talk to and instruct yourself.

Chapter Three

Getting Stuck

Recently we were talking to our friend and colleague Alison about a leadership idea we both agreed was brilliant, instructive and helpful. Alison was so inspired and energised by the idea we described that she asked who had come up with it. However, on hearing the name of the management guru responsible, her face fell and her pleasure evaporated.

"What's the matter?" we asked.

"It just so happens," she explained, "that I saw that person speaking at a management conference last month. He was dreadful – low-key, low-energy, dry, uninspiring; it was the most boring session I've ever seen. I hated it."

"Wonder what happened?" we asked.

"It was like he was stuck in his analytical deep-thought mode. You know, the mode he must be in most of the time when he's researching, thinking and writing down these great ideas. He was delivering his presentation in that gear and he put us to sleep."

Getting stuck in one distinct collection of behaviours seems to be a common occurrence. We notice it in our ourselves…

- when we're not getting the result we want
- when we're not creating the impact we're after
- when we're not making the sale we'd hoped for.

There are famous examples from history – this one is as recent as 2005:

> **"Gordon – you really must talk more slowly.**
>
> "The relentless pace and volume of the Brown delivery makes me feel as if I'm being run down by a super-charged steamroller. I'm not alone: fellow listeners shared similar feelings with me afterwards, as they have following other Brown speeches. Less would be more. Some breathing spaces, a few shifts of register and tone, a sense of being in conversation with your audience rather than hectoring them like a Victorian hellfire preacher…the humanity and warmth that Gordon Brown can show in private conversation seems to fade in direct proportion to the number of people he is addressing."
>
> Timothy Garton Ash, *The Guardian*, 16th December 2005

Getting stuck in one gear makes sense; when you have a set of behaviours that works well for you and brings you success in your chosen pursuit it's likely that you'll use this set of behaviours over and over again. It's possible that you'll learn to fall back on that set of behaviours in more than one situation – in more than one environment. Sooner or later, it's possible that you'll have learned to use this set of behaviours so well that you'll automatically slip into it in all kinds of situations, whether or not it's appropriate – like slipping into autopilot without realising you've done so.

Dam it, not again!

Then there's another kind of getting stuck. Sometimes we observe people (and ourselves) getting stuck in a gear that's *been* working in *the* situation so far, but suddenly, for whatever reason, it stops working.

You probably know the kind of thing we're talking about: when you get into your stride with a set of behaviours that seems to be getting the response or result you want. So, you stick with it and, all of a sudden, for the other people you're with, that set of behaviours becomes…

Too fast   Too aggressive   Too brash   Too intense
Too straight

or

Too soft   Too slow   Too gentle   Too laid-back
Too easy-going   Too humorous

What productive behaviours do you get stuck doing?

And it's not just management gurus, political interviewers and high-profile politicians who have these experiences. We see it in some very ordinary situations.

We'll be watching a manager with someone in an interaction that's fast, serious, detailed and direct, and it's working well – the manager's behaviours are helping the person to think differently. Helping them to commit and putting them under productive pressure to do something. Then, quite suddenly…

It's too much.

The person has had enough of this full-on experience. Because the interaction has been good so far, both participants can afford to ease off. But, by this point, the manager is much too strongly 'in their stride' – they're so involved and so deep inside their own thinking and their own agenda that they don't even notice that something's changed. As things change further – as the person they're with becomes less responsive – the manager becomes more desperate to get the result they felt they were getting before. They carry on – in fact, they may even intensify their behaviours further. They get stuck. And the other person starts to get stuck, too.

If you're not already, you could be thinking about:

How I get stuck   Who I get stuck with

The other day, Mark experienced such a phenomenon at a class he attends regularly as a learner. As the class began, it became clear that the instructor had been on some further training for himself the previous week. He's always strong, challenging, opinionated and intense; Mark likes the clarity this usually brings to the class. The training he'd received the previous week had evidently stoked him up – it had been some kind of positive wake-up call for him. With no introduction, he challenged the group to demonstrate what they'd learned in previous weeks. Great! This woke the group up and shocked them out of their slow start.

Once they'd all completed their demonstrations, he began to lecture the group. He asked challenging questions about their practice, all the while maintaining a straight and serious face. Mark hadn't turned up in a great state himself on this morning and the shock therapy was focusing him – helping him realise he wasn't managing himself and investing enough in this development (which he's chosen to do).

Other members of the group weren't so happy with the approach – but the instructor has a good connection with the class, built up over many weeks of interaction, and he was ramping up his personal impact with them to push them into a different learning state. So, it was a risk, but one worth taking for the learning outcome.

But he kept going. He worked himself into a groove of passion and intensity. The group stood listening to what became a rant – again fine, except that the rant went on…

and on…

and on…

Something that Mark had appreciated for the first five minutes became a turn-off for him when it was still going 10 minutes later. By now the instructor was making the same points over and over. Those who had turned off during the first five minutes were shuffling and looking down at their feet like naughty children. Mark became bored and his thoughts drifted off – the opposite of the productive focus produced in the first five minutes of the session.

Next the instructor picked out one of the group to work with in the centre of the room, in front of everybody else – a normal and usually helpful occurrence. Unfortunately, on this occasion, he remained in the same gear. In this one-to-one interaction, the intensity and passion became harrying, strident and unforgiving. If there hadn't already been sufficient levels of rapport and understanding between the group and the instructor, we could easily have misconstrued what we were watching as bullying.

Remember, this instructor is a highly skilled and very accomplished individual who does great work with this class. He just got stuck in a particular gear on this day, lost his connection with them and became a bore while he was at it.

Please don't judge him harshly. This happens more often than any of us might like to think. We've done it ourselves many times over the past 20 years. That's why we started noticing our gears – that's why we've written this book.

The following week, the instructor had addressed all of the above. He was still focused and intense, but he'd changed down to a less passionate, simpler, stripped-back, quieter, softer gear. He taught specifics in a gentler manner and left the group to try them out in pairs. It was a perfect complement to the week before and it worked a treat as a contrast.

At the end of this second session, he found the right moment to describe how this week he'd had a word with himself before beginning – being clear with himself to talk less and make sure he didn't become too preachy. That's right! He'd consciously been working on his gears – consciously completing a Pre-Check beforehand and using it to warn himself about his tendency to go too far with some of his best behaviours and ramp them up into too high a gear for too long!

He even had a label or a name for this too-high gear. He said it himself: "Preachy."

Chapter Four

Only a Metaphor

About now, it's possible you're flinging this book aside, shouting your objections:

It's too mechanical

This isn't how people work

I'm not this robotic

We agree with these objections – people don't work in the mechanical fashion we're describing. This 'gears' thing is only a metaphor. We're not trying to describe a truth when we talk about gears – we're just trying to give us a simple way of thinking about ourselves and our behaviour.

Changing gears is a metaphor designed to help you quickly recognise the kinds of shifts in behaviours you have available to you, understand where you normally get stuck and identify sets of behaviours that you want to develop – need to develop – because you don't have those sets of behaviours easily available to you at the moment.

In defining your own gears, you'll have available a simple way of noticing what's happening in particular situations and what's going on in situations where you're not getting what you want.

Once you begin to play with this metaphor, you'll be asking yourself simple questions that immediately make sense and help you identify what to do differently.

Connection questions like…
- What gear am I in?
- What gear are they in?
- Which gear would get a better response?

Promoting alertness in others questions like…
- How long have I been in this gear?
- Are they losing interest?
- Which gear should I switch to?

Personal impact questions like…
- What gear am I in?
- What response do I want from them?
- Which gear from me would communicate that?

Promoting alertness in myself questions like…
- How long have I been in this gear?
- Am I losing energy?
- Which gear should I switch to?

Once you've been playing with this metaphor for a while, you'll find that just one of these questions is often enough for you to make the changes you need immediately (without having to do much more thinking).

Chapter Five

Defining a Person's Gears

Let's get to it!

We find it best to define someone's gears in terms of a few simple polarities:

- Slow to fast
- Easy-going to high-intensity
- Warm to cold
- Gentle to tough
- Informal to formal

- Saying a little to saying a lot
- Superficial to overly detailed
- Quiet to loud
- Low energy to high energy
- Accommodating to challenging

It's difficult to be too prescriptive about exactly how to define *yours*; you'll need to follow a logic that works for you. But what we're after is a way of defining to yourself the manner in which your behaviours might progress, e.g.

From lower gears	to higher gears
Easy-going	More intense
Slower	Faster
Warmer	Colder
Gentler	Tougher

Some people don't seem to want or need such a straightforward progression. It's up to you to work out what makes the best sense.

To define your gears, consider at least three questions:

1   What are the different sets of behaviours that I already know I display on most days, e.g. when I'm at work?

2   What are the gaps between these sets of behaviours – gaps which suggest sets of behaviours I could use to make interactions/ communications different or better?

3   What are the different sets of behaviours that I want to be able to display, but currently don't seem to do often or very naturally? It's likely that these new sets of behaviours will be prompted by one of the reasons to change gears listed in Chapter Two:

Once you begin to think about the sets of behaviours you seem to fall into frequently, you'll notice some of the extremes you use (extremes in terms of some of the above polarities – slow to fast, warm to cold, etc.). As you start to recognise these extremes, some sets of behaviours that you think are missing will become obvious.

For example, when we look back at when we began working together, we both think that Mark had got fixed in a very particular set of gears in the workplace – pretty much as follows:

Gear	Name	Qualities
1st		
2nd		Quick, verbal, fun, sarcastic, silly, witty
3rd		Sensible, straightforward, logical
4th		
5th		Cool, methodical, detailed, direct, analytical, pushy, uncompromising, at my pace, action-oriented, incisive, high-energy, straight
6th		
7th		Cold, blank, clinical, robotic, remorseless, pushy, fast, incisive, analytical, controlling, nitpicky
8th		

As you can see, while Mark's behaviours weren't exactly one-dimensional, they were not particularly well rounded. At that time, Doug was less fixed in the sets of gears available to him in the workplace. He often made use of a similar 'sensible, straightforward, logical' gear to Mark's third gear and this was the one that helped us connect. But many of his other usual gears were warmer, more easy-going and less intense than Mark's.

Mark had strong personal impact, which was getting him to places he wanted to go. He was pretty good at promoting interest in himself via creating difference. He was influential, but in a particular way and in a limited set of circumstances. In truth, he wasn't good enough at promoting alertness and interest in others via difference. He wasn't good at connection with easy-going, friendly types. He wasn't good at connection with people who didn't want to think so hard and for so long – people who need to lighten up and have a good laugh sometimes. He was often asked to give people feedback because he was so happy to tell it like it is, not hold back and challenge people with precise information about them and their behaviour.

So, while he was skilled at cranking out good work, he'd lose people along the way sometimes. He would sometimes induce responses in them like "leaves me cold". Some would respond similarly to the way *The Guardian* writer responded to Gordon Brown: a feeling of "being run down by a super-charged steamroller". Some would report how much they valued his ability to challenge them to think, then challenge them again and again: a bit like a dose of cod liver oil – you sort of know it's good for you, but it's not enjoyable.

Equally, things between us didn't go so well at first. Doug stopped driving to meetings with Mark because he'd usually leave with a headache.

Some of the feedback baffled Mark and people who knew him well, but he decided to do something about it anyway. Somehow he felt he was misrepresenting himself – that in work situations people weren't getting to 'play' with the real him.

When we first looked at Mark's gears together, we could see the gaps between the sets of behaviours he typically used. He could see there was a set of behaviours missing at the lower end of the continuum – not a gap between gears, but the realisation that he typically started in a higher gear than some people found helpful or comfortable. There was a lighter, more easy-going set of behaviours that should come even *before* his lowest fun, silly, witty gear. When trying to build rapport and establish a good connection with some people, his fun, silly, witty gear just didn't do the job (and neither did his more intense, speedy, challenging behaviours). Meanwhile, as a starting point, his sensible, straightforward, logical gear was just boring.

Furthermore, he realised that once he got down to business there was typically no let-up – he would get stuck in his higher gears. There was no light and shade to keep people's interest – there was little warmth and little enthusiasm later on (instead, there was passion and intensity) and, again, little in the way of easy-going behaviours.

You might have other suggestions about what might be missing between Mark's gears, based on how you like to work with people.

Chapter Six:

Starting to Think About Your Own Gears

Think of a situation you're familiar with: maybe your interactions with someone who works for you, a customer or your boss – someone you don't feel you're getting on with as well as you'd like. Think about some typical interactions you've had with them.

1   Reflect on your behaviours. Notice what *you* are like…
  - at the beginning of your interaction – when you greet each other.
  - in the middle – when you get down to business, getting on with whatever it is you're meeting for.
  - at the end – when you're drawing conclusions and finishing off.

2   Now consider issues of `Connection` or lack of `Connection`. Reflect on what *they're* like by comparison…
  - at the beginning.
  - in the middle.
  - at the end.

3   Next, consider issues of `Promoting alertness and interest *in others*`. Ask yourself if there's a particular groove *you* get into – a particular energy you settle into during the interaction. Consider the behaviours you're using that typify this groove.

4   Finally, consider issues of `Personal impact` – how to move conversations on so that things happen, things change and you make progress with what you're trying to do together.

Keep paying attention to differences between what you're like and what they're like in response (this will help you identify where your behaviours are on the polarities we've mentioned, e.g. by comparison with them, you might realise you're cooler and less smiley).

Look at the words listed on the next page. They'll help you to start describing your gears to yourself – they're not intended as a comprehensive list, so don't be limited by them. Identify qualities you would cluster together to describe what you're typically like at the beginning, middle and end of an interaction.

	Name	Qualities
Beginning		
Middle (down to business)		
End		

Have a look back at examples of Mark's gears on the previous page if you want to see how the progression *might* work.

Creative	Demanding	Involved	Certain
Excited	Unforgiving	Long-winded	Manipulative
Direct	Specific	Curt	Inexpressive
Straightforward	Scientific	In your face	Grounded
High-energy	Uncompromising	Busy	Overbearing
Positive	Conciliatory	Loud	Minimalist
Risk-taking	Emotional	Brash	Abrasive
Persuasive	Sympathetic	Slow	Cutting
Listening	Forgiving	Upbeat	Remorseless
Decisive	Passionate	Realistic	Talkative
Warm	Submissive	Careful	Silent
Friendly	Boring	Gentle	Expert
Arrogant	Upright	Harsh	Advising
Analytical	Thinking	Brash	Sleepy
Candid	Open-minded	Abrasive	Empathetic
Sarcastic	Interrogating	Honest	Disinterested
Ruthless	Protective	Quiet	Loving
Brutal	Alert	Clinical	Showing Integrity
Wishy-washy	Assertive	Robotic	Cautious
At coachee's pace	Unstoppable	Caring	Controlling
At my pace	Chatty	Incisive	Supportive
Relentless	Lucid	Questioning	Nice
Can't say no	Insightful	Shoulder to lean on	Reactive
Small-talky	Fun	Belligerent	Proactive
Rude	Furious	Passionate	Easily distracted
Detailed	Miserable	Clumsy	Focused
Objective	Expressive	Gregarious	Cold
Resilient	Theatrical	Organised	Attentive
Determined	Provocative	Process-led	Dismissive
Critical	Methodical	Investigative	Aggressive
Task-focused	A pushover	Reluctant to	Patronising
People-focused	Weak	commit	Overbearing
Pushy	Strong	Incomprehensible	Fast
Dominant	Aloof	Nitpicky	To the point
Bright	Detached	Cluttered	Vague
High-energy	Interested	Trusting	Blank
Reflective	Rigorous	Conscientious	Can do
Plodding	Showy	Methodical	Can't do
Action-oriented	Data-oriented	Blinkered	

Chapter Seven

Naming

It's going to help to name your gears. This will enable you to instruct yourself more quickly and directly when you realise something you're doing is not working and it's time to change (we call this moment a Time Out). It's not helpful to have to start working your way through all your behaviours (slow down, move less, get quieter, etc.) – this really would produce a mechanical performance from you. Instead, it can be easier to give yourself one instruction – a name that captures the theme or the sense of the gear you might adopt next to help the communication.

Remember the example of Gordon Brown – "Super-charged Steamroller" could have been the name of one of his gears. Then there's the leadership guru our friend Alison heard presenting – he seemed to be stuck in his Research Nerd gear when he should have been using his Entertaining Guru gear.

It can also help before a communication begins – we call this a Pre-Check. It can help you consider which gears you want to be ready to use (again, without a too specific behaviour-by-behaviour analysis).

Remember the class instructor that Mark experienced who accidentally drifted into his Preachy gear – in his Pre-Check, he could have directed himself to be ready to change down into his Relaxed Coach gear.

Look at the clusters of qualities you've listed at the beginning, middle and end of an interaction, and consider what name you might give to each one.

Here are Mark's again, as listed above, but this time with the names he gave them:

Gear	Name	Qualities
1st		
2nd	Fun/nonsense	Quick, verbal, fun, sarcastic, silly, witty
3rd	Straightforward	Sensible, straightforward, logical
4th		
5th	Challenging	Cool, methodical, detailed, direct, analytical, pushy, uncompromising, at my pace, action-oriented, incisive, high-energy, straight
6th		
7th	Interrogator	Cold, blank, clinical, robotic, remorseless, pushy, fast, incisive, analytical, controlling, nitpicky
8th		

Chapter Eight

Filling in the Gaps

As described in an earlier chapter, even before fully understanding what was going on, we identified that there were gaps: missing gears for Mark. We didn't actually know what behaviours were missing but, even before we worked out the specifics, it was useful to identify that the size of the jump between one set of Mark's behaviours and another was just too big – too jarring for other people to receive. These jumps are the gears you can see are left blank in the table above. It felt like when Mark progressed from one set of behaviours to another there were big leaps in qualities such as intensity, and big shifts in qualities such as warmth.

And, as described earlier, it also seemed evident just from a look at Mark's gears that we knew there was a lower gear missing – a more gentle, easy-going, warm set of behaviours.

Think about your own gears now. Consider the ones you began to identify a few pages back and then:

1 Consider that there might be a missing earlier, lower gear than the one you logged as the typical beginning of your interaction.

2 Consider that there might be other sets of behaviours in between the middle and the end (and even after the end). This will help you identify some further sets of behaviours that may be missing – not so much because the other person needs them from you, but because the size of the jump in behaviours from one to the other seems too big.

Just check what other sets of behaviours this starts to suggest you may typically be under-using at the moment.

	Name	Qualities
Beginning		
Middle (down to business)		
End		

Chapter Nine

Changing Up for Personal Impact

Doug was working with a client in a retail organisation – a regional director (RD), managing a team of store managers. For this RD, visiting her stores was a regular key opportunity to review progress, agree new targets and objectives, and coach the team through the delivery of these targets.

As the visit progressed, Doug noticed a number of things that might be useful to discuss with the RD about her performance and her particular style in working with a store manager.

At an appropriate moment he called a Time Out with her and reviewed the visit so far. The RD thought the visit was going well – "a good productive interaction" – but, at the same time, she had the feeling that she wasn't really getting enough from the store manager. When Doug asked her what she wanted, she said she wanted more certainty from the store manager in the answers he was giving, more detailed thinking and more get-up-and-go regarding his business.

These two people had been in this manager/report relationship for years; they seemed comfortable with each other and they knew how their interaction would go. As a result, the RD was: supportive, understanding, warm, friendly and easy-going.

Throughout the interaction, she led with her own ideas and her own thinking on the topics under discussion. As a result, the store manager wasn't being asked to do much thinking and certainly wasn't being challenged to identify how he could move his business on and develop new opportunities. It was a pleasant, inoffensive interaction that kept the commercial situation ticking over.

Once Doug had heard the RD's perceptions of how the visit was going and what she wanted to be different, he asked her a few simple questions:

"How many gears do you have?"

"I'm sorry," she said. "What do you mean?"

"Well," Doug explained. "When I say gears, I'm thinking about levels of speed, toughness, intensity, challenge...and so on. How many gears do you have? Three? Five? Six? Eight? What do you think?"

The RD thought for a few moments. "Six," she replied.

"And how many gears have you used in this visit so far?"

The RD took a sharp intake of breath and winced. "Oh, right..." she said. "Probably one or two at the most."

"All right," Doug said. "Let's work out what those gears have been."

After a few minutes of discussion, they concluded together that the gears she'd used so far could be characterised as:

- Gentle, warm, humorous, friendly behaviours;

and

- Fair, reasonable, thoughtful, interested, advisory, "This is what I think..." type behaviours.

Next Doug asked whether the RD would describe these as low or high gears.

"Low," she concluded.

"And if you were to step up a gear or two, to get what you want – more certainty, more detailed thinking and more get-up-and-go – what would you be like?" he asked.

The RD came up with a brief list of characteristics: challenging, questioning, analytical, pacier, quieter and "I'll say less".

Doug asked if this collection of behaviours was a gear of its own. The RD agreed it was.

"So what would the gear above that one be?" Doug asked.

The RD thought about it for a while, looking at the words Doug had written down in front of her. Then she listed the qualities she thought would indicate a further change of gear upwards: tough, fast and direct.

Doug suggested she concentrate on her third gear – challenging, questioning, analytical, pacier, quieter and "I'll say less" behaviours.

He was clear that he didn't want her to let go of the two gears she'd used so far in the visit: the gentle warmth and the fair and reasonable advice. What he wanted her to do, though, was to focus her attention on her third gear.

As the RD resumed the visit, the change in her was subtle but immediate. Sharper, less accommodating – more forward energy. She asked more questions and filled the gaps with her own ideas less. As a result, she paid more attention to the store manager. She was more challenging.

At the end, the RD asked the store manager what he thought of the visit. "It was great," he said. "You've really made me think about my business differently. You're a really nice person. You always give me a good visit, but today you challenged me to get clear about how I'm going to drive the business. And, what's more, I am clear. The changes you got me to identify in the last department are really good. They'll definitely add sales."

"What was different about the way I conducted the visit?" she asked.

"You got me thinking more than usual. You didn't accept my first answer – you were far more challenging than you've been before."

"How do you feel about that level of challenge?" asked the RD. She was worried – she had to know.

"I feel fine," the store manager said with a big grin. "That level of challenge is good for me."

Chapter Ten

One Discipline with Two Names

Once you've identified the gears you have, there's a personal discipline that's required in order to make use of what you know. It's a thinking discipline – one which is useful to consider at two distinctly different parts of any communication. We've given it two different names.

Just before the communication begins, we call it a Pre-Check.

Then…multiple times, throughout the communication – we call these Time Outs.

Both are intended for you to sort yourself out so that you can communicate more effectively, depending on which of the usual objectives you're after:

Connection

Personal impact

Promoting alertness and interest *in others*

Promoting alertness and interest *in yourself*

You might think that this is all a bit too obvious to bother with. That's a great point – it *is* ridiculously obvious. But because of the way human attention works, even though it seems obvious, it's not something that many of us do naturally. Many of us are so busy focusing on the content of a conversation or the task we're working on that we only pay fleeting attention to our own behaviours (or the behaviours of others), and usually only afterwards, when we notice that the conversation didn't go the way we wanted it to.

The exception is when people are nervous, when they're going into an obviously high-pressure situation or when they perceive that there's something significant at stake. Then they tend to pay more attention to their behaviours – they focus more on selecting the most suitable ones. But even this doesn't stop them from getting fixed; because they're so tense, they can easily, accidentally, select only one set of behaviours.

Of course, it's precisely because a Pre-Check/Time Out doesn't suggest itself naturally when there's no pressure that it *is* a discipline – something that you need to make happen, whether you feel the need for it or not.

Chapter Eleven

The Pre-Check

Before a communication begins, you don't know how the people you'll be communicating with will respond to you (obviously), so the Pre-Check discipline is an estimate – an estimate of the behaviours you *might* need based on what you know about the people you're going to be with. We're hoping that, as a result of this little book, you'll be estimating the gears you *might* need to combine in order to achieve the quality of communication you want – *to connect, achieve impact or promote interest.*

The important word in the above statement is 'might'. An estimate doesn't always turn out to be correct. During the Pre-Check, you're estimating behaviours you *might* need to use. You're not fixing yourself to use them whatever happens. This is important because some gears should only be 'switched on' in response to what's happening. So the Pre-Check is about preparing yourself to use them without getting yourself fixed that you *will* use them.

Why bother? When a behaviour isn't a habit, it's difficult to switch it on, i.e. it's difficult to vary your behaviours beyond your habitual range. Technically, more accurately, your habitual behaviours are waiting deep in a very ancient part of your brain and they'll emerge spontaneously in response to situations – they'll literally crowd out non-habitual behaviours.

One way you can make this less likely is to make yourself ready to use some non-habitual behaviours. Just identifying that you need to be ready to use certain behaviours – giving yourself permission – makes the likelihood of using them greater. This is what the Pre-Check does for you – it increases your ability to be flexible; it increases your ability to use non-habitual behaviours if and when you need to.

Chapter Twelve

Time Out

The Time Out discipline is the same but different. Use this discipline to keep an eye on your own behaviours while your communication proceeds. Because of the way the human attention system works, this won't happen automatically. Our focus drifts naturally to the task in hand, or the content of the conversation, rather than the behaviours being used.

But expert communicators consciously keep themselves focused on their own behaviours – in relation to the situation, in relation to others or in relation to their objective. Expert communicators regularly push their attention back to their own behaviours for a few seconds to assess whether they need to adjust them. For most of us, this isn't a natural way of doing things, which is why Time Out is a discipline. The good news, though, is that once you've used it enough as a discipline, it can become something you naturally do, i.e. it's a skill you can develop.

"I did stand-up comedy for eighteen years. Ten of those years were spent learning, four years were spent refining, and four were spent in wild success. My most persistent memory of stand-up is of my mouth being in the present and my mind being in the future: the mouth speaking the line, the body delivering the gesture, while the mind looks back, observing, analysing, judging, worrying, and then deciding when and what to say next. Enjoyment while performing was rare – enjoyment would have been an indulgent loss of focus that comedy cannot afford."

Steve Martin, *Born Standing Up – A Comic's Life*, **2007, Simon & Schuster, p1**

Chapter Thirteen

Changing Down for Connection

Mark was working with two coaches, helping them develop their coaching skills further. As part of the process, he asked them to coach each other while he observed.

What was obvious immediately was how good they both were in the various skills and behaviours of coaching. They both demonstrated great listening, great questioning, the ability to notice what was being said and what wasn't being said…and so on.

They were quite different in the typical behaviour patterns (or gears) they seemed to prefer using. The distinction was best demonstrated in a particular session. The coach in this instance seemed to be settled into a pattern of behaviours, which were: logical/rational, low and controlled energy, cool, confident, mechanical, rigorous, high-intensity, high-challenge, relentless thinking, focused, inquisitive, methodical, detailed and analytical.

If you're reading this and thinking "Yuk!" then we should say that, observing these behaviours, they seemed to Mark, in isolation, to be very useful and it was clear the coach's intention was positive and helpful.

But the context of the session was that the person being coached usually seemed to settle into a different pattern of behaviours, with qualities such as: intuitive and emotional, variable and expressive energy, warm, confident, gentle and caring, rigorous, low-intensity, mid- to high-challenge, structured, focused, interested, methodical, detailed and fun.

You should be able to get an immediate picture of what might happen if you compare these qualities side by side.

Logical/rational	Intuitive and emotional
Low and controlled energy	Variable and expressive energy
Cool	Warm
Confident	Confident
Mechanical	Gentle and caring
Rigorous	Rigorous
High-intensity	Low-intensity
High-challenge	Mid- to high-challenge
Relentless thinking	Structured
Focused	Focused
Inquisitive	Interested
Methodical	Methodical
Detailed	Detailed
Analytical	Fun

As you can see, the coach and coachee shared a lot of typical qualities or behaviours, but there were also some key differences that would affect their interaction.

When the session was finished, Mark reviewed how it was for each of them. The coach was pleased with her performance and described the great questions she'd used, how much had been discovered and how much she'd helped her partner move on during the session.

The person being coached agreed with this analysis, but said she had not enjoyed the session very much and had difficulty remembering the specifics of what she was going to do as a result of the coaching. On further questioning, she explained that something about the whole thing had given her "the creeps" and left her "cold".

During the session, Mark had written down all the questions in the order they were used – like a full script for their interaction. He offered to try another session with the same coachee while the person who had been the coach observed.

What Mark didn't tell either of them was that he was simply going to repeat the session, using the script of the same questions and the same structure, but that he was going to pay attention to his gears to increase his levels of warmth, gentleness and care while he did so.

Once they'd finished, Mark asked both of them for their feedback. The person who had been the coach previously was very complimentary about the questioning and the structure (Of course! It was the one they'd used). The person being coached was incredibly excited. "That was the best coaching session I've ever had!" she said.

Mark was shocked at just how greatly her response had changed when he'd actually repeated so much of the previous session (we continue to be shocked on regular occasions at how little it takes to move a situation from one place to another entirely).

During the first session, the coach had been using productive behaviours, which in many cases would have got her a good result (and usually did). In this particular situation, though, with this person, she was in too high a gear and needed to change down more regularly in order to stay with her partner.

Many people say to us things like: "It's all very well, but what if I haven't met the other person? What if I don't know the behaviours that the other person is going to respond best to? I can't do a Pre-Check then, can I?!?"

In this situation, the Pre-Check is designed to keep you flexible. The Pre-Check isn't so much about the other person and what *they're* going to be like; it's more about what you notice about yourself – how you typically get fixed into particular gears.

The Pre-Check is your opportunity to give yourself a good talking to about this: "Now, listen, you know what you're like – you can be a bit full-on; you can get too intense and logical/rational too quickly. Make sure you listen early on – make sure you wait – don't get too excited too early. Be ready to use your lower chatty/small-talky gear – gentle, warm, interested – if that's needed. Be ready for your gentle/fun gear – enthusiastic, warm, interested – if that's what's needed – wait until you feel that the connection is good enough."

Your Pre-Check can help you manage the emergence of too much one-dimensional behaviour and allow you to pay attention to what's going on for the other person involved.

After this, you can keep using little Time Outs to make quick decisions about what's needed and which bits of your estimate (Pre-Check) you need to make use of.

In this example, the coach could have used her Pre-Check to acknowledge how she tended to become fixed in her 'Robot' gear – logical, rational, cool behaviours, which probably work really well for her on most occasions, but which needed to be assessed for effectiveness this time. She could have used a number of Time Outs during the session to assess whether this Robot gear was working *for* the coachee or whether she needed to turn up other gears, which she'd considered during her Pre-Check.

Chapter Fourteen

Considering New Gears You Might Develop to Change Up or Down

Take a look back at your own gears – those you've started to identify so far, both in relation to someone else's behaviours and in relation to the gaps between your existing gears.

Now, based on what you've read about changing up for personal impact and changing down for better connection, consider what sets of behaviours you could adopt that would be a shift up or a shift down in intensity, speed, volume, etc. from what you've already got. Again, the words are available on the next page to help you consider what might help with the person you have in mind.

	Name	Qualities
Beginning		
Middle (down to business)		
End		

Creative	Demanding	Involved	Certain
Excited	Unforgiving	Long-winded	Manipulative
Direct	Specific	Curt	Inexpressive
Straightforward	Scientific	In your face	Grounded
High-energy	Uncompromising	Busy	Overbearing
Positive	Conciliatory	Loud	Minimalist
Risk-taking	Emotional	Brash	Abrasive
Persuasive	Sympathetic	Slow	Cutting
Listening	Forgiving	Upbeat	Remorseless
Decisive	Passionate	Realistic	Talkative
Warm	Submissive	Careful	Silent
Friendly	Boring	Gentle	Expert
Arrogant	Upright	Harsh	Advising
Analytical	Thinking	Brash	Sleepy
Candid	Open-minded	Abrasive	Empathetic
Sarcastic	Interrogating	Honest	Disinterested
Ruthless	Protective	Quiet	Loving
Brutal	Alert	Clinical	Showing Integrity
Wishy-washy	Assertive	Robotic	Cautious
At coachee's pace	Unstoppable	Caring	Controlling
At my pace	Chatty	Incisive	Supportive
Relentless	Lucid	Questioning	Nice
Can't say no	Insightful	Shoulder to lean on	Reactive
Small-talky	Fun	Belligerent	Proactive
Rude	Furious	Passionate	Easily distracted
Detailed	Miserable	Clumsy	Focused
Objective	Expressive	Gregarious	Cold
Resilient	Theatrical	Organised	Attentive
Determined	Provocative	Process-led	Dismissive
Critical	Methodical	Investigative	Aggressive
Task-focused	A pushover	Reluctant to	Patronising
People-focused	Weak	commit	Overbearing
Pushy	Strong	Incomprehensible	Fast
Dominant	Aloof	Nitpicky	To the point
Bright	Detached	Cluttered	Vague
High-energy	Interested	Trusting	Blank
Reflective	Rigorous	Conscientious	Can do
Plodding	Showy	Methodical	Can't do
Action-oriented	Data-oriented	Blinkered	

Chapter Fifteen

Captivating communicators know just how to flex their energy, seriousness and warmth to increase the power of what they're saying. They know that to really 'land' an intense and serious message, they may need to follow it by lightening up and smiling for a moment. They know somehow that if they're telling a really funny story and everybody around them is laughing, they should pause and wait while the audience laughs. They know that they may need to laugh themselves for a second and wait for the audience to catch up, rather than just ploughing on with the telling.

Captivating communicators know that if they're ranting, shouting about something they feel passionate about, they may need to quieten down and slow down for a few moments as a way to increase the intensity and emotion the audience is feeling. If they just carry on ranting, it might have the opposite effect and decrease that intensity.

Great communicators somehow pick the one or two best gears to use to communicate a combination of passion about their topic and appropriate emotion (to match their topic or match the audience's emotional response – similar to pausing for the laugh).

If you watch a number of Ted Talks in a row, you'll be able to categorise the performances in a number of ways in relation to gears:

1   Those where the content is just so good it doesn't matter whether the speaker is varied enough.

2   Those where the speaker has picked the right couple of gears upfront (in their Pre-Check) and uses them to remain interesting throughout, even when the content isn't so riveting; somehow they make subtle gear shifts at little moments and keep us with them.

3   Those where, even when the content is good, the speaker is not varied enough. The talk is bland (i.e. the speaker should change gear more to keep our attention).

4   Those that get mentioned in various lists of the most annoying or worst Ted Talks; often, particular words crop up in the descriptions of these speakers, which betrays how they've somehow got stuck in a gear, e.g. "conceited", "boring", "waffling", "unvarying", "a bit dull", "took forever to get to his point" and a "muted harangue of self-regard".

If you watch a number of these talks in a row and begin thinking about people's gears, it doesn't take many to start to see the differences.

What's interesting is that these are well rehearsed, carefully written talks with content that's specifically designed to be interesting in a short period of time. So you might be surprised that speakers still get it wrong with their gears in this forum. Remember, it's easily done – we're all human. Take a look at a few examples that illustrate different things.

Monica Lewinsky: The Price of Shame
Monica Lewinsky selects a limited number of gears upfront – maybe only one gear, but it's the right one for the content. And, of course, the content is so strong and impactful that this is a good example of a performance that remains interesting throughout *without* the need for gear changes. Nevertheless, as you watch, notice if there's

a point where you personally would like a different gear from her – a lightening, a softening, more anger – whatever. It's only 22 minutes, but even in such a short piece you might notice your attention dipping at some point. **https://www.ted.com/talks/ monica_lewinsky_the_price_of_shame**

Shane Koyczan: To This Day... For the Bullied and the Beautiful

This guy's a poet and poetry is not to everybody's taste, but he changes gears multiple times – using three or four different collections of behaviours to deliver a captivating performance. The apparently easy-going manner with which he begins coupled with the many changes of tone, emphasis, volume, speed and smiling/ non-smiling gestures are probably conscious choices. The stepping into the characters of the story he tells and then the lift of volume and emphasis in the latter stages, moving into ranting and even shouting (a much higher gear), getting away with it all to keep us fascinated – these are all conscious gear-change decisions. **https:// www.ted.com/talks/shane_koyczan_to_this_day_for_the_ bullied_and_beautiful?**

Kelly McGonigal: How to Make Stress Your Friend

So many conscious minute-by-minute shifts in tempo, expression and tone ensure this potentially dry, deep and intense subject matter remains riveting. This is a conscious performance showing off the use of many gears (we didn't count – we were too busy watching and listening). Sometimes she speeds up for one or two sentences to get to the next point. Once in a while she slows right down and emphasises a point. She moves from smiles to a straight face and back to smiles. She holds silences, lets the audience laugh, smiles with them, changes facial expressions for emphasis and moves from all this into a more consistently straight face when she gets to the serious messages she wants us to remember. **https://www.ted.com/talks/ kelly_mcgonigal_how_to_make_stress_your_friend/discussion**

There's no doubt that speakers like these have done their Pre-Checks and, if you watch carefully, you'll be able to spot the Steve Martin-like Time Outs each takes in order to keep judging the situation and what gearing to use.

Consider again whether you're able to make such tiny momentary shifts into different gears when you're in the zone like these speakers (remember the management guru we described in Chapter Three – the one who was stuck in one very dry, cerebral gear only and didn't make any of the necessary small shifts we can see from these communicators to keep our friend Alison interested and engaged).

We get to work with people on presenting and public speaking quite a bit. What often surprises people is that even relatively moderate levels of variation in tone, pace and pitch, which expert speakers show, have taken practise – sometimes lots of practise.

Many of us assume instead that excellent performers and speakers are just doing what they know how to do naturally. On the contrary, great speakers and performers often consciously develop their ability to shift gears, change pace and so on. There are surprising and strange photographs of Adolf Hitler practising many of the dramatic (sometimes outlandish) poses and actions that he used in famous speeches he made. Yes, even evil dictators consciously put work in to develop more gears to influence their audience and keep them engaged while they rant at them. **https://rarehistoricalphotos. com/hitler-rehearsing-speech-front-mirror-1925/**

Chapter Sixteen

Considering More New Gears

Have another go – now in the context of your ability to change up or down in order to maintain the interest of your listeners.

	Name	Qualities
Beginning		
Middle (down to business)		
End		

Chapter Seventeen

Practise

OK, so by now you've identified a number of gears that you want to be able to switch on. Some of them you'll know just how to do. With a little conscious effort, you'll already know how to do the behaviours involved – and you'll be able to switch them on just by instructing yourself to use that gear, naming that gear e.g. Straightforward, Fun/nonsense, Super-charged Steamroller, Relaxed Coach, Entertaining Guru, Evil Dictator, etc.

With others, of course, you'll be thinking that you don't know how to do the behaviours involved, that you've never done them before and that you don't know where to begin.

This is trickier. And there's a trap involved – which many of us fall into.

There are several simple things you can do, but either you won't want to do them or, as soon as you begin, you'll object and justify to yourself why you should stop.

First, here are the simple things you can do:

1   Rehearse the new behaviours with someone who knows you well. Get them to help you find a way to do them – and find a way to do them in a way that's suitable for you. But don't concentrate on making it suitable for you immediately (this is part of the trap).

2   Rehearse new behaviours in front of the mirror. This seems difficult, but it can work (remember, it worked for Hitler – he rehearsed all kinds of outrageous, over-the-top poses, which he then got away with at countless rallies and events).

3   Find the feeling in you that accompanies the behaviour you want; e.g. if you need to smile more, you should concentrate on your sense of the comic, which usually makes you smile. This isn't the same as imagining comic, funny or stupid things happening when you're in an interaction that requires the behaviour from you – this could lead you to smile in all the wrong places in the interaction. Instead, it's about finding the amusing, slightly comic things that crop up during an interaction – instructing yourself to notice them and allowing yourself to pause when they happen, focusing on them properly and giving yourself the time and space to respond to them with a smile (rather than pressing on with your own thoughts and communication because that's where your focus is), i.e. just slowing down.

Smiling for a photograph isn't the same as smiling in response to somebody else or in response to something amusing – it's a different part of the brain that's used. So, if you learn just to force a smile for the sake of some manipulative behaviour, it'll never look like a real smile (because it isn't). Instead, change the focus of your attention from your own agenda and behaviours to the funny things that crop up in conversation. Allow yourself time and space to smile about them – then it will be genuine.

Chapter Eighteen

Now for the Trap!

When you're trying to switch on unfamiliar or new behaviours, it's particularly important for you to be aware of two parts of your brain:

- The prefrontal cortex – the thinking brain. It's the part of your brain just behind your forehead and literally the container for 'what's on your mind'.
- The basal ganglia – this is a cluster of cells in the mid-brain, within a much older part of the organ – quite literally between your ears.

Habitual behaviours sit in the basal ganglia – once they're there, it's thought they stay there forever. And once they're there, they feel comfortable. This is because the basal ganglia is a deep-seated and old part of your brain that performs behaviours unconsciously – effortlessly.

By contrast, when you learn a new behaviour or try an unfamiliar one in a different situation from usual, those behaviours are performed by the prefrontal cortex. Your brain is literally thinking its way through the behaviours as you do them.

So, when you use a new or unfamiliar behaviour, you perform it with the part of your brain designed for thinking it through – which is appropriate for learning. But it's not the part of your brain designed for habits. Because of this, the new behaviour will feel clunky, unnatural, false, lacking authenticity or not genuine. You're literally thinking it through, rather than performing it naturally.

The problem? There's only one way to move the behaviour from the prefrontal cortex to the basal ganglia: repetition!

The trap: as soon as you try to use a different or new behaviour, you immediately report how unnatural and clunky it is…

It doesn't suit me

It's not authentic

It's just not me

And then you stop using it. And you're right: the new behaviour doesn't suit you…not yet! Of course it's not authentic! It's new – it's all these things because you haven't used the behaviour enough (you haven't even used it at all). You need to give your brain time and practise to find the right way to do it for you. It's a bit like starting to learn a musical instrument, a new sport or a new dance and giving up immediately because it doesn't feel natural. You don't really believe that Jimi Hendrix was born playing electric guitar. "It's a boy, Mrs Hendrix. Listen – he's playing the electric guitar!"

You'll have to repeat your new behaviour and practise it quite a lot of times before your brain will do it comfortably for you. The good news is that some behaviours take as few as three repetitions to move to the habit centre, but for others it will take more – many more. But even twenty-five or fifty repetitions isn't a lot of minutes of practise in front of a mirror. It's not that difficult or time-consuming – you just have to stop moaning and get on.

Most people spend the time available to them explaining how the new behaviour is clunky and doesn't feel authentic when they should just shut up and get on with the practise and repetition needed.

The famous economic historian and Harvard professor of economics John Kenneth Galbraith described it more succinctly this way: "Faced with the choice between changing one's mind and proving that there is no need to do so, almost everyone gets busy on the proof."

Adopting a new set of behaviours requires you to change your mind – you have to shift the position of the behaviour from new brain to old brain. But many stop the practise required to do so with the objection that the behaviour is wrong for them.

That's the trap.

Don't fall for it.

Chapter Nineteen

Keeping *yourself* alert and productive is difficult. If you're stationary for long periods of time, looking in the same direction, using the same or similar thinking processes, your thinking brain may begin to struggle. Your mental energy may start to wane and your physical feelings of energy and alertness will wane along with it.

Too much different stimulation – chopping and changing the focus of your attention – is not good for your stress levels. On the other hand, too little difference – not enough variation, not enough stimulation – is not good for your stress levels either. Sitting in the same situation, allowing yourself to *blob* into a lethargy of mind and body isn't good for you and your mental or emotional state.

As a result, it's useful for your sense of personal productivity, your sense of well-being and your personal stress levels to make sure you shift gears even when there's nobody else present. In short, the effect of awakened interest that your behaviours can produce in others is similar – or the same – as the effect they can produce in yourself.

This particular use of changing gears is different from the rest. It's possible it'll require you to define a second smaller set of gears so that you know what you need to do for yourself. Furthermore, the discipline of Time Out is essential to this use of changing gears. Nothing will happen unless you take regular moments to notice what state you're in in the first place. The difficulty is that, across the day, as you sink into an energy slump of lethargy, tiredness, negativity, etc. you'll be less likely to take the Time Out required. As we've said before, this is why Time Out is a discipline – a thinking activity you do regularly, whether you feel the need to or not.

It's now known that talking to yourself out loud isn't necessarily the first sign of madness; it's a valid way to help you think differently. It's a valid way to focus your thinking – and a particularly valid way to help you with problem solving. So talking to yourself out loud could be a gear that you could use.

If you get more familiar with the types of gears you get yourself into in a typical working day, then, when appropriate, you can have a conversation with yourself to shift into a different one.

For example, if you can become more familiar with your:

- I'm too stressed gear
- I'm too comfortable gear
- I'm too slow gear
- I'm too analytical gear
- I'm indecisive gear
- I'm unfocused gear
- I'm distracted gear
- I'm too tired gear

And their counterparts:

- I'm decisive
- I'm fast
- I'm focused
- I'm alert
- I'm talking out loud to myself

And so on…

Then, when you're trying to increase your productivity, or when you're trying to reduce your stress, you can direct yourself. You can give yourself clear instructions on how to switch from one set of behaviours to another.

Mark often does this – he has a fast, focused, hard-working, decisive gear. He calls it his High Production gear. He's now so familiar with it that, sometimes, when he's dawdling, procrastinating or just being plain lazy and unfocused, he tells himself to sort it out – usually this involves him concentrating on moving faster and ignoring things like emails and texts. Sometimes this is enough to shift him into a High Production state where he gets loads done. Once or twice a month, he'll mention this as part of the conversation: "So then I shifted into High Production gear and I had a great day."

Sometimes not…

We didn't say it was easy, did we?

As usual, your first step is to have a go at defining a number of gears that relate to this kind of thing. Use the table below to try this for the first time. If you don't know where to begin, try using some of the headers listed above to get you going – i.e. define your stressed gear, your distracted gear, etc. Then, once you've detailed some of the behaviours that accompany them, you can switch your description to the alternatives – even the opposites.

Examples of the gears Mark refers to here:

	Name	Qualities
	Procrastinating	Distracting myself with my phone or guitar. Chatting. Indecisive. Slow. Dawdling. Not settling on one piece of work or another.
	Clearing out	Doing small jobs. Making decisions. Sending emails without much thought. Going too fast to overthink things.
	Organising	Calm. Rational. Considered. Planning. Chunking my time – e.g. emails for 20 minutes, phone calls for 20 minutes, big projects for 40 minutes.
	High Production	Decisive – which big piece of work am I doing now? Ignoring emails. Ignoring texts/ messaging apps. Tunnel-visioned. Moving to a different workspace.

Define your gears here:

Chapter Twenty

Good Luck – Remember, These Aren't Really New Gears

So there it is. We could go on – there's so many examples and situations in which this idea is relevant. But the idea itself is simple and basic, albeit challenging to adopt. If you've got this far, we don't want to get stuck in a gear ourselves and risk boring you.

The key is to identify the gears you want based on the objective that you've identified:

Connection

Personal impact

Promoting alertness and interest *in others*

Promoting alertness and interest *in yourself*

But also recognise that the new behaviours that you want are not necessarily that *new*. Many of the gears you want to develop may be available in other parts of your life. Working with people on their behavioural flexibility over the last twenty years, we've noticed a curious but understandable phenomenon: most of us already have many different gears, but we keep them partitioned off from each other. For example, we unconsciously keep our 'pub' behaviours in the pub and our 'with my boss' behaviours with the boss. But, in our experience, the walls between these different gears are only partitions and we can remove them.

So once you make conscious choices about the behaviours you need to use to smooth transitions between your current gears, to connect better with people, to increase your impact or to create and maintain interest levels, you might find that you've already got them available. After this, it's just a matter of consciously giving yourself the instruction to use them. And, remember, that's what the Pre-Check and Time Outs are for. Or it may be just a matter of consciously putting in the practise to use them in different situations.